PAIDEIA MONOGRAPHS

SOUL & BODY

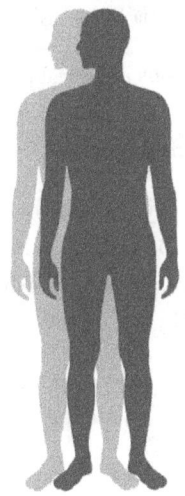

D.F.M. STRAUSS

PAIDEIA
PRESS

www.paideiapress.ca
www.reformationaldl.org

Soul and Body

This monograph edition is a publication of Paideia Press (3248 Twenty First St., Jordan Station, Ontario, Canada L0R 1S0). Copyright ©2020 by Paideia Press. All rights reserved.

Except for brief quotations in critical publications or reviews, no part of this book may be reproduced in any manner without prior written permission from Paideia Press at the address above.

Unless otherwise indicated, Scripture quotations are from the ESV® Bible (The Holy Bible, English Standard Version®). Copyright © 2001 by Crossway, a publishing ministry of Good News Publishers. Used by permission. All rights reserved.

Paideia Monograph Series Editor: Steven R. Martins

Book Design by: Steven R. Martins

ISBN 978-0-88815-266-4

Printed in the United States of America

Contents

The Dialectical Split between Body
and Soul: Its genesis in Greek culture ... 6

    Plato ... 7

    Aristotle ... 9

The Medieval Synthesis ... 17

    Augustine ... 17

    Thomas Aquinas ... 18

    Complications for the anthropology
of Thomas Aquinas ... 22

The Dialectical Root of Modern Philosophy ... 27

Towards an Alternative View ... 33

    Habermas Rejects a Naturalistic
Reductionism ... 35

    Implications of a Biblical Perspective ... 36

    Supra-Temporality ... 44

Concluding Remarks ... 48

Literature ... 53

About the Author ... 59

SOUL & BODY

Transcending the Dialectical Intellectual Legacy of the West with an Integral Biblical View?[1]

Abstract

Greek philosophy informed the Medieval dualistic understanding of "body" and "soul" which continued to influence modern Humanism and Christian views during and after the middle ages. These fluctuating conceptions express the directing role of dialectical basic motives. It was mainly the Greek motive of matter and form which directed the thought of Plato and Aristotle, resulting in a dualistic view of the relationship between a so-called *material body* and *rational soul*. At the *Council of Vienne* (1312) the Aristotelian-Thomistic doctrine of the soul as the *substantial form* of the

---

1. Paper presented at "The Soul Conference," Oxford, 28 June – 1 July 2013. This work is based upon research supported by the National Research Foundation.

body was adopted. Within Protestant circles the "two substances" view caused a distinction between a (temporal) material body and an (eternal) rational soul (see article 7 of the Swiss *Confessio Helvetica Posterior* and the *Westminster Confession* Chapter IV, paragraph 2). Dooyeweerd shows how modern philosophy has received its deepest motivation from the dialectical motive of nature and freedom which informed the development from Descartes up to Gould and Jaspers. Finally, in the last sections, the main contours of a biblically informed view is articulated with reference to the centrality of the human I-ness, to the theory of enkaptic interlacements and to the problem of supra-temporality.

The Dialectical Split between Body and Soul: Its genesis in Greek culture

SINCE ITS INCEPTION Greek philosophy struggles with the dialectical tension between the transitional world of becoming and the urge towards incorruptibility. Sometimes other opposites are employed, such as the *limitless* and the *limited*; the *constant* and the *changeful*; *matter* and *form*. What is special about this kind of dialectic is that the two poles both threaten and presuppose each other. Within the development of Greek culture this split eventually results in the view that the human being is constituted by a rational soul and a material body. Thompson provides a clear account of the relationship between body, mind and soul in the thought of Plato and Aristotle (cf. Thompson, 2012:14).

Plato

In the context of the fear for death the discussion leader in Plato's dialogue *Phaedo* proposes to get an answer to the question: "For what sort of thing should we fear this fate, and for what should we not?" (Phaedo 77b). In search for an answer to this question Plato relates "what is always constant and invariable" to what is "incomposite," and "what is inconstant and variable" to what is "composite." What Plato has in mind is the status of his transcendent ontic forms (*eidè*). Plato distinguishes between the visible and invisible in terms of the invariable and what is never the same: "So you think that we should assume two classes of things, one visible and the other invisible?", followed by specifying the question: "The invisible being invariable, and the visible never being the same?" Plato then claims that the "body would have the closer resemblance and relation" with the visible, while the "soul is more like the invisible" (79c ff.). Therefore in this dialogue Plato argues that rational thinking is directed at what is invisible and constant. The visible and changeable, by contrast, can only be observed through the senses. He further explains this split by referring to an absolute reality which remains "always constant and invariable" and then asks: "Does absolute equality or beauty or any other independent entity which really exists ever admit change of any kind?" The alternative contemplated here is captured in the question: does "each one of these uniform and independent entities remains always constant and invariable, never admitting any alteration in any respect or in any sense?" (78d).

The explanation emerging from the on-going conversation anticipates the problem of positivism, which wants to restrict science to "sense data," but then fails to account for the status of the terms employed in describing what has been observed by the senses. Plato distinguishes sensory objects from those entities that are constant: "And these concrete objects you can touch and see and perceive by your other senses, but those constant entities you cannot possibly apprehend except by thinking; they are invisible to our sight" (78e).

In the light of these views it is not surprising that Plato repeatedly relates the distinction between soul and body to the distinction between what is constant and what is variable.

> The soul is most like that which is divine, immortal, intelligible, uniform, indissoluble, and ever self-consistent and invariable, whereas body is most like that which is human, mortal, multiform, unintelligible, dissoluble, and never self-consistent (80b – translation by Hugh Tredennick, 1966:132).

Aristotle transforms the theory of ideas of Plato, and in doing this he continues to provide his own dynamic to the development of the Western intellectual legacy. Ernst Fischer remarks: "First Aristotle is translated, then he is ordered, subsequently he is subjected to commentaries, later on he is interpreted, soon he is criticized, sooner or later he is refuted, sometimes he is despised, and so it always proceeds until our contemporary situation, which is still strongly involved with Aristotle" (Fischer, 1996:15).[2]

Aristotle

Aristotle commences with a primary substance as signifying unit, designating "that which is individual." However, he immediately introduces a "secondary substance" which "is not an individual, but a class with a certain qualification, since words like "man" and "animal" are "predicable of more than one subject" (Aristotle, 2001:12 – Categoria 3b10-18). Hartman discerns a close connection between concepts and universality in Aristotle's thought, although initially it was not as-

---

2. "Erst übersetzte man ihn, dann ordnete man ihn, anschließend kommentierte man ihn, später interpretierte man ihn, bald kritisierte man ihn, irgendwann widerlegte man ihn, ab und zu verachtete man ihn, und so geht das immer weiter bis in unsere Gegenwart hinein, die immer noch stark mit Aristoteles beschäftigt ist und nach wie vor durch den selbst Unbewegten in Bewegung gehalten wird."

serted. To this he adds the remark that knowledge of a particular involves universals: "Aristotle does not say at first, as one might wish him to say, that even true belief presupposes a facility with concepts and therefore universals; but he does not shrink from the conclusion that knowledge of a particular (or, as he sometimes seems to mean, of a matter of fact concerning a particular) involves universals" (Hartman, 1977:21). Whereas Plato's ideas do not depend upon their participants for their existence, Aristotle's "universals do depend on their instances" (Hartman, 1977:22). For this reason what is recognized as particular still has to be of a "certain sort": "if it is entirely unique, nothing can be known about it" (Hartman, 1977:25). Having started with his (purely individual) primary substance, Aristotle knows he has to introduce something universal in order to secure the knowability of a substance. At the same time, in his *Metaphysics*, he realizes that there are serious problems involved in relating what is individual to universality and to knowledge:

> The statement that all knowledge is universal, so that the principles of things must also be universal and not separate [individual] substances, presents indeed, of all the points we have mentioned, the greatest difficulty, but yet the statement is in a sense true, although in a sense it is not (Metaph. 1087a10-15 – Aristotle, 2001:911).

In line with this view Aristotle, in *De Anima*, also considers the primary substance to be *unknowable* because knowledge is only possible of the *universal essence* of things, which, as we noted above, is designated by Aristotle as the *secondary substance*, the *to ti ēn einai* (cf. *De Anima*, 412b16; cf. 414a9-11 – Aristotle, 2001; 556 and 558).

For Aristotle true knowledge is therefore ultimately knowledge of the *general form*. In the third Chapter of the seventh Book of his *Metaphysics*, Aristotle articulates the negative implications of his stance by subtracting all positive determinations of being, thus rendering matter as such *unknowable*. Not only does he deny all positive determinations of being in respect of matter, for even negating them does not hold for matter (*Metaph.*, 1029a24-25).

The absolute formless matter functions as the limit point of all negative designations. We are therefore here justified to discern a true *via negativa* in the conception of Aristotle. In his extensive work on matter in Aristotle's thought, Heinz Happ goes beyond the *protē hulē* (primary matter) to what he considers to be Aristotle's *highest matter principle*, "matter as such": "The distinction between *prima materia* and 'Hulē-Prinzip' is nowhere explicitly made by Aristotle, and yet it follows necessarily from his argumentations" (Happ, 1971:696-

697). It may appear as if Happ reaches this conclusion by acknowledging both the *positive* and *negative* designations of matter. Since the designation *primary matter* still contains a positive affirmation ("primary"), Happ plays it off against Aristotle's negative approach. On the basis of this ambiguity he then concludes to the *highest matter principle* of Aristotle. Of course Happ does not realize that for Aristotle it is one and the same matter which allows for approximating positive knowledge while negating conceptual determinations causes matter *as such* to escape from being conceived.

Moreover, matter as such finds its counterpart in its dialectical opposite, pure, *actual form*. Pötscher formulates it precisely when he explains that Aristotle understands his god in such extreme terms that it "at once appears in pure dialectics as opposite, as the negation of what is material" (see Pötscher, 1970:51). Ter Horst captures this ultimate dualism as follows: "For Aristotle *matter* is an eternal principle of movement and change, and of an unlimited transition of the one into the other; the *form* is likewise an eternal principle of enduring being, and of limitation to generic determination" (Ter Horst, 2008:28). Verdenius and Waszink note that the principle of *dūnamis* and *enērgeia* rests on *protē hulē* [primary matter] as a more fundamental principle – the "ultimate substratum of all transformation" which "never *exists* except *qua* determined by some form" (Verdenius and Waszink, 1968:57).

Potency and *act*, instantiated as *matter* and *form*, are eternal, supra-temporal and nongenerated principles of whatever there may be. Yet these principles must be mutually related, although there is no theological necessity to reduce the one principle to the other since the god of Aristotle, who is equated with the *pure act*, is no Creator and therefore not the absolute origin of what is.[3]

Of particular importance in this regard is the fact that the Aristotelian conception of the relationship between the universal essence (universal substantial form = secondary substance) eventually turns out to be the starting-point of the medieval (in particular: Thomistic) understanding of the relationship between the (material) body and the (rational) soul. According to Aristotle, substance could be understood in two senses: as the ultimate substratum, persisting through

---

3. "Potentie en akt, geinstantieerd als materie en vorm, zijn eeuwige, boventijdelijke en ongeworden beginselen van al het zijnde. Deze beginselen moeten wel op elkaar worden betrokken, doch er bestaat geen theologische noodzaak het ene beginsel oorzakelijk tot het andere te herleiden. De God van Aristoteles, die met de zuivere akt wordt gelijkgesteld, is geen Schepper, en dus geen absolute oorsprong van het zijnde" (Ter Horst, 2008:29).

all changes and as the form furnishing a "this" with its distinct meaning. Hartman explains: "Matter is the subject of predication; form is what makes a substance what it is, and is therefore at least a necessary condition of the substance" (Hartman, 1977:29).

Aristotle combines the relationship between matter and form with the difference between potentiality and actuality. He states categorically: "Now, matter is potentiality, form actuality; ...the *body* cannot be soul; ... Hence the soul must be a substance in the sense of the form of a natural body having life potentially within it. But substance is actuality, and thus soul is the actuality of the body" (*De Anima*, 412a10-23 – Aristotle, 2001:555).[4] Therefore, a substance is constituted by a principle of *potency* and a principle of *activity* which, in the case of being human, are represented by *body* and *soul*.

The way in which Aristotle conceives of his understanding of substance takes into account two different issues, namely the relationship between universality and what is individual and as well as the relation between persistence and alteration (constancy and change) – both problems to which Plato responds in his own peculiar way. Hartman points out that Aristo-

---

4. For a more detailed discussion of Aristotle's notion of the *Psuchē* as form, see Everson, 1991:171 ff.

tle appears to believe that even Heraclitus holds that "there is some sort of stuff that abides through all change" (Hartman, 1977:28-29) – which is one of the conditions set by Aristotle for being a substance. On the next page he adds that a substance, according to Aristotle, must be *something*, having form and belonging to a species, "for only if it is such can it undergo certain changes and still remain what it is."

In his above-mentioned recent penetrating work on the deconstruction of the principles of form and matter in the ontology and epistemology of Thomas Aquinas, Geert der Horst first explores the Greek background of the problem and within this context provides us with a brief summary statement of the successive responses to the problem of being and alteration (constancy and change). The issue is: "How can we say that something *is* if experience teaches us that everything constantly changes?" Ter Horst characterizes the responses as follows:

> The solution of Parmenides and to a lesser extent of Democritus is to reduce becoming to being. The solution of Heraclitus is to reduce being to becoming. Plato's solution is to maintain both becoming and being by assigning them to different domains. Finally, the solution of Aristotle is to attempt to maintain both by unit-

ing them in a very peculiar way (Ter Horst, 2008:68).[5]

In his extensive multi-volume work on "Reformation and Scholasticism in Philosophy," Herman Dooyeweerd distinguishes between theoretical designs (what Thomas Kuhn called *paradigms*) on the one hand and the underlying ultimate commitments that give direction to theoretical views of reality on the other. He designates the latter also as *religious ground-motives*.[6] In the first Volume of this work he provides a brief

---

5. "De oplossing van Parmenides en in mindere mate van Democritus is om het worden te herleiden tot het zijn. De oplossing van Heraclitus is om het zijn te herleiden tot het worden. Plato's oplossing is om zowel het worden als het zijn te behouden door ze over verschillende domeinen te verdelen. Aristoteles' oplossing tenslotte poogt beide te behouden door ze op een heel bepaalde wijze met elkaar te verenigen."

6. However, we should keep in mind that within the Dutch language it is possible to distinguish between the radical, central and integral meaning of religion, touching the heart of being human, and all the issues of life proceeding from this core dimension. Amongst these differentiated articulations, faith and confessional activities are found alongside all the other issues of life (see Proverbs 4:23). In English, the word *religion* is normally used only to designate the *faith function* of reality. Therefore one should distinguish between religion in a *functional* (aspectual) *sense* and religion in its life-encompassing *radical and integral sense*. (Radical here means: *touching the root of human existence*; and integral means: *embracing all of life*.)

characterization of the ancient Greek basic motive of form and matter, the biblical ground-motive of creation, fall and redemption, the medieval (synthesis) motive of nature and grace and the modern humanistic ground-motive of nature and freedom (see Dooyeweerd, 2012 – see pages 1-20).[7]

The Medieval Synthesis

The attempted synthesis between the Greek ground-motive and the biblical ground-motive provides the basis for long-standing dualistic views of reality and the human person. The development of Greek philosophy does not reconcile the two ultimate (but opposing) principles of origin of matter and form. The only option is to assign primacy to one of the two poles. During the medieval era the influence of the Greek motive of form and matter not only informs a dualistic understanding of reality but also a dualistic understanding of being human.

Augustine

According to Augustine God did not create matter without form (Augustine, 1982:1, 15). Later on, in his *Confessiones* (Augustine, 1966:XII, 6), when he explains

---

7. The Aristotelian-Thomistic legacy is analyzed in the Second Volume of *Reformation and Scholasticism in Philosophy* (see Dooyeweerd, 2013).

that formless matter is formed concurrent with its creation, the crucial question remains unanswered: is formless matter *created*? Whenever Augustine approaches matter in its absolute formlessness, it hides itself in utter darkness which can only be approximated by employing negative determinations (Conf. XII, 6, 6), similar to when it is defended that one can only say what God is *not* (a negative-theological stance). In order to be faithful to the biblical creation motive it is affirmed that matter is created, but not in its formlessness. The underlying tension reveals itself in the following dialectical formulation: by creating matter (which is distanced from God) God reaches the limits of its power (*Conf.* XII,7,7). This shows that the formless matter approximates the *nihilo* (nothing) of the idea of *creatio ex nihilo* (creation out of nothing), demonstrating that the "nothing" after-all is "something (evil)." Clearly, since matter is not created without form the "nihilo" brings to expression the after-effect of the (depreciated) *matter* motive of Greek philosophy. The same legacy is found in Augustine's *Confessions* where the empty and desolate earth (Gen. 1:2) is depicted as *formless matter* (Augustine, 1966:XII, 3).

Thomas Aquinas

That Thomas Aquinas is dependent on both Aristotle and Neoplatonism explains why he characterises God as the *primary form* (*prima forma exemplaris*) of all things that participate in Him.[8] From this Kremer concludes that "the ipsum esse per se subsistens becomes the arch-image of all forms and as such the original image of all beings. ... And if it is already the Form of forms, then every form derives from it, just as all beings do. Every being is then nothing but a limitation of this Form of forms, manifesting it in a bounded and limited way without limiting the Form of forms."[9]

Aquinas struggles with the biblical revelation regarding creation because he continues the Greek (Platonic-Aristotelian) view on the first or primary matter (*prima materia*). An investigation of this issue shows that he solely relates substances constituted by form and matter to God's act of creation. As a result, Aquinas does not speak in creational terms of *primary matter*. In his *Summa Theologica* (Aquinas, 1945:I, 44, 2), in the third Objection, Aquinas argues that it is against

---

8. So for example in his commentary on Dionysius's *De Divinis Nomibus*, no. 631.

9. Kremer argues this point with extensive references from the works of Thomas. Compare also pages 356-357 where Kremer indicates that God, according to Thomas, is (in a Neoplatonic sense), the "utmost general/universal" (the 'Allerallgemeinste'). Kremer summarizes it: "Since whatever is outside God somehow has to participate in this Form, it [God] in fact becomes 'forma formarum' and 'Idee der Ideen' [the 'Idea of ideas']" (Kremer, 1971:316).

the nature of matter, which exists only potentially, to be created. However, in his Reply he responds by arguing that the Objection does not show that matter is uncreated, but merely that it is not created *without form*.[10] Also in *his Summa Theologica* (Aquinas, 1945:I, 15, 3) Aquinas alleges that matter is created by God, but not without form.[11] It is nonetheless repeatedly argued in his *Summa contra Gentiles* (S.c.G.) that God (as *actus purus*) brought everything into existence without prior matter.[12] These statements do not solve the problem, for the question is whether the formless primary matter was created in its formlessness? When Aquinas argues, at the end of S.c.G. II,16, that since God is the cause of all things (*causa omnium*), he is also the cause of primary matter (*Deus igitur est causa materiae primae*), he still does not provide a direct answer to this question. A consideration of the mentioned statements of Aquinas from S.Th. suggests that a direct answer in S.c.G. also should be that God did not create (first) matter without form. That is to say that God did not

---

10. "Dicondum quod ratio illa non ostendit qoud materia non sit creata, sed qoud non sit creata sine forma."
11. "Sed quia nos ponimus materiam creatam a Deo, non tamen sine forma."
12. "Producit igitur Deus res in esse sine matria praciacente" (Aquinas, 1982:II, 16).

cause first matter without form.[13] In itself matter does not display being and it is also not knowable.[14]

Matter continues to represent pure potentiality. According to Aristotle and Thomas Aquinas, form is the uniting factor within a substance. Yet, as Ter Horst points out, the fact that *form* cannot communicate a true unity of being to matter is related to the above-mentioned problematic view of Thomas Aquinas, namely that God cannot bring matter into being without form (see Ter Horst, 2008:53). The underlying dualism operative in all of this entails that only the *compositum*, the substance composed out of form and matter, comes into being and passes away, for neither matter nor form as such is subject to coming into being and passing away. Ter Horst explains that since primary matter is formless no idea (form) of it can be conceived, implying that God does not have an idea according to which he could have created it.[15] Alternatively Thomas Aquinas holds that potency is co-cre-

---

13. Problems in Thomas's conception of creation are also extensively discussed by Sertillanges (1954:363-420) and by Manser (1935:509-549).
14. S.Th. 1, 15, 3: "Nam materia secundum se neque esse habet, neque cognoscibilis est."
15. He mentions Lib. LXXXIII, quaest. 46 where we read: "sed materia prima nullam habet formam; ergo idea in Deo nulla ei respondet" (Ter Horst, 2008:73).

ated (*concreari*) with what primarily has been created, namely substance (see Ter Horst, 2008:74).

God does not contain anything potentially and therefore His essence coincides with His being. He is pure activity (*actus purus*) and therefore *being* essentially applies to Him who is "ipsum esse per se subsistens" (see Aquinas 1945:I.44.1c and Aquinas 1982:II,15, 16).

Complications for the Anthropology of Thomas Aquinas

Since Thomas accepts the view of Aristotle regarding the composite nature of the human being as substance, his view of the ontic unity and individuation of the composite substance (of body and soul) wrestles with serious problems. Combining act and potency (soul and body) entails a threat to the unity of being of the substance, because matter cannot be subsumed under the unity of form. Ter Horst explains the problem: "Matter in its potentiality has its own being independent of the form and with that independent of the substantial *compositum*. However, such an independent being of one of the principles of the substance inevitably abolishes the unity of the substance. The substance which is composed out of form and matter also does not have a true *individuality*, because flowing from its complete potentiality, matter without form cannot be a principle of individuality, whereas the form can communicate to matter only a generic being, not an individual being, and with that to the *compositum*" (Ter Horst, 2008:79).[16]

Plato, with his dualism between the intelligible world of static ontic forms and the sensory world of becoming (*genesis*) does not advance the view that the human being is composed of two substances, namely matter and form. Although he criticizes Plato's view Aristotle neither takes matter nor form to represent an independent substance. However, the subsequent medieval developments lead to the Thomistic struggle with the idea of a *compositum*, of a two-substance understanding of the human being. But once body and soul are seen as substances, the question arises how the resulting substantial unity could be reconciled with two independent substances (body and soul)?

It should be kept in mind that the traditional scho-

---

16. "De materie bezit in haar potentialiteit een eigen zijn, onafhankelijk van de vorm, en daarmee onafhankelijk van het substantiele compositum. Een onafhankelijk zijn van een der substantiele beginselen heft echter onvermijdelijk de eenheid van de substantie op. De uit vorm en materie samengestelde substantie heeft ook geen ware individualiteit, daar de materie wegens haar volledige potentialiteit geen individuatiebeginsel kan zijn zonder de vorm, terwijl de vorm alleen een soortelijk zijn, geen individueel zijn, aan de materie, en daarmee aan het compositum, kan meedelen."

lastic view regarding the relationship between body and soul proceeds from the conviction that the soul is "indestructible."[17] This conviction has its foundation in the psycho-creationist conception. While Thomas Aquinas accepts the active *nous* as being implanted from the outside he in addition has to take into consideration the church doctrine regarding the rational soul (anima rationalis) as a simple substance, accompanied by the psycho-creationist view according to which the soul must be created by God separately within the human body. Since the activity of the *rational soul* is independent of the body, the soul is viewed as existing by itself as a spiritual substance which nonetheless is an *incomplete* substance.

Aquinas therefore struggles with the status of the human soul and its apparent borderline existence between bodily substances and separate substances. Natural things are substances "composed out of matter and form" (Aquinas, 1982;65, 281). Repeatedly Aquinas posits the problem: can a spiritual substance (substantia intellectualis) be united with a body as its form? (see Aquinas 1982:289, 295, 403, 457).

---

17. In Chapter 55 of the first part of the *Summa contra Gentiles* (ScG) it is asserted that every intellectual substance is *incorrruptible* ("omnis substantia intellectualis est incorruptibilis" – see Thomas, 1982:215).

The problem is how something subsistent could be a substance without ending up with a substance *within* another substance? The task formulated by Thomas Aquinas is to investigate how a spiritual substance could be united with a body?[18] He aims at accounting for the way in which a spiritual substance ("substantia intellectuali") and a body could essentially be united (become one – ScG 56; Aquinas, 1982:229). Oftentimes the issue is stated in terms of the question whether a spiritual substance ("substantia intellectuali") could be the *form* of a human body.

In the first article of his *Questio disputata de anima* a distinction is made between a strict and a less strict manner in which something could be subsistent and then he classifies the human soul as less persistent. Yet, ultimately the incorruptibility of the soul causes Aquinas to opt for the view that a human being "is composed from a spiritual and corporeal substance."[19] Although the phrase *substantia corporalis* only occurs once in the ScG of Aquinas, the conception is present throughout this work. In passing we may note that since Aquinas accepts the Aristotelian view (*Metaph.* 1074a 34) that

---

18. "restat investigandum utrum aliqua substantia intellectualis copori possit uniri" (ScG 56; Thomas 1982:225).

19. *Summa Theologiae*, I, Q. 75: "De homine, qui ex spirituali et corporali substantia componitur."

"all things that are many in number have matter" there cannot be a multiplicity of form substances, because they are supposed to be without matter.

According to Dooyeweerd these tensions are the embodiment of the impossible attempt "to achieve a synthesis between the Scriptural motive of creation and the Greek form-motive" (see Dooyeweerd, 2013:344). He here also points out that the Thomist view implicitly obtained its official ecclesiastical confirmation at the *Fifth Lateran Council* chaired by Pope Leo X (c. 1513–17), and he reminds us that already at the earlier *Council of Vienne* (1312) the Aristotelian-Thomist doctrine of the soul as the *substantial form* of the *body* was adopted (Dooyeweerd, 2013:345).

In summarizing the Greek legacy it is clear that Aristotle transforms Plato's transcendent ontic forms into the (universal) substantial forms of material bodies, without being able to escape from the ultimate dualism of *matter* and *form* as principles of origin, also reflected in the dualism between *potency* and *act*. He only considers the combination of form and matter as constitutive for the substantial unity of the human being. Although Plato already argued for the incorruptibility of the soul, Aristotle rejects the idea of the immorality of the soul – a feature attached only to the active reason (*nous* – which is not a soul) which operates from the "outside" in order to become active within human thinking. Hence neither Plato nor Aristotle advances the idea that the human being is composed of *two* substances, body and soul. Within the developments of the medieval era it was the Church doctrine of the indestructibility of the human soul that resulted in the Thomistic view which accepted these two substances (body and soul).

Protestant theology continues the "two substances" view by distinguishing between a (temporal) material body and an (eternal) rational soul (see Calvin, Inst. Book I, Ch XV:2) See also article 7 of the Swiss *Confessio Helvetica Posterior* and paragraph 2 of Ch. IV of the *Westminster Confession*.

The Dialectical Root of Modern Philosophy

Since the Renaissance modern humanism has proceeded from the ideal to be *free* and *autonomous*. For this purpose it has explored the possibilities of the modern natural sciences, supposedly capable of explaining reality entirely in terms of exact natural laws of cause and effect. In this way a new dialectical basic motive has emerged, namely the motive of *nature* and *freedom*, also known as the *natural science ideal* and the *personality ideal*. A dialectic similar to the Greek basic motive of *matter* and *form* and the medieval motive of *nature* and *grace* now gives direction to the development of modern philosophy. From the outset an ultimate antinomy accompanied this development, for if everything is determined by the exact (physical) law of cause and effect, then human freedom also has to surrender to it. This is already seen in the thought of Descartes, who commences by postulating two mutually irreducible substances, *res extensa* and *res cogitans* (the extended substance and the thinking substance), for it turns out that in the final analysis Descartes does accept an interaction between "soul" and "body" owing to the operation of a small gland, the *parva glandula* (the pineal gland). This view paves the way for Spinoza, Hobbes and Leibniz to explore the primacy of the nature motive.

In the thought of Hobbes, for example, the human soul is reduced to a mechanism of feelings in motion. Rousseau starts to assign primacy to the freedom motive: "Nature commands every animal, and the brute obeys. The human being experiences the same impulse, but recognizes the freedom to acquiesce or to resist; and particularly in the awareness of this freedom the spirituality of humankind manifests itself" (Rousseau, 1975:47).

After his study of Galileo's *Dialogues*, Thomas Hobbes deepens his conviction that the only reality is that of *motion*. During his stay in the French capital he entered into a polemic with Descartes concerning the latter's separation of soul in terms of mechanistic arguments. Ultimately the materialistic metaphysics of Hobbes subsumes the soul in all respects "under the category of a moving body" (see Dooyeweerd, 2012a:243-250). This dominance of the nature motive (science ideal) is only curtailed by Immanuel Kant who transforms the distinction between essence and appearance (derived from the Greek concept of substance), into his own distinction between appearance and thing-in-itself, which is motivated by the nature-freedom (Sein-Sollen) dialectic: "For if appearances are things in themselves, freedom cannot be saved" (Kant, CPR-1787:564 – he calls the human soul a "thing-in-itself").

The motivating influence of this dialectic in the basic motive of nature and freedom causes a negative understanding of freedom: it is always conceived as freedom from *natural necessity*. George Herbert Mead clearly understands how this motive initially has given rise to the dominant *mechanistic* tendency in modern physics since Galileo. In his *The Philosophy of the Act* we read: "The concept of nature which was introduced by Galileo through his doctrine of dynamics, reduced it to a statement of matter in motion" (Mead, 1945:357). He realized that this doctrine, has reduced reality to "extended matter in motion" thus discarding the possibility of "mind" because it denies the existence of so-called *secondary qualities* (such as color, sound, warmth, taste as well as the affective properties of things) (Mead, 1945:358-359).

As a contemporary of Mead, Merleau-Ponty develops his own articulation of this basic dualism. He largely relies upon the results of psychological and psycho-pathological studies. Thus the dialectic of nature and freedom assumes its own form in the thought of Merleau-Ponty. He explores two basic denominators, namely *bodyliness* (in a biotical sense viewed as an *organism*) and *existence* (which for him is *historical* in nature). In following Sartre, he on the one hand holds that "I am my body." On the other, however, he is convinced that a person's historical existence must *repress* the bodily organism to the pre-personal level of an *anonymous organic complex*.[20] The following two quotations respectively represent the sentiments of the natural science

---

20. Note the difference between the views of Merleau-Ponty and the meaning attached to the term "organism" in the thought of Aristotle. According to this meaning every branch at once originates, exists and passes away with all the others, implying that a truly living entity is neither divisible nor is it composed of parts – it is united by its substantial *form*. The view, dating back to Aristotle's definition of the soul, causes a misunderstanding of the word "organikon" – see the discussion by Bos (2003:85 ff., 93-94, 107-108, 162, 174 and 200).

ideal and the personality ideal:

> I cannot understand the function of the living body except by enacting it myself, and except in so far as I am a body which rises towards the world (Merleau-Ponty, 1970:75).

and

> ...so it can be said that my organism, as a pre-personal cleaving to the general form of the world, as an anonymous and general existence, plays, beneath my personal life, the part of an *inborn complex* (Merleau-Ponty, 1970:84).

The dialectical situation is clear: On the one hand, I *am* my body, and on the other my body is seen as a pre-reflexive, pre-personal, anonymous complex by virtue of its being-in-theworld (Merleau-Ponty, 1970:79, 80, 82, 83, 86). *Nature* and *freedom* mutually *threaten* and *presuppose* each other:

> ...for most of the time personal existence represses the organism without being able either to go beyond it or to renounce itself; without, in other words, being able either to reduce the organism to its existential self, or itself to the organism (Merleau-Ponty, 1970:84).

His thoughts jump dialectically to and fro between these poles:

> Man taken as a concrete being is not a psyche joined

to an organism, but the *movement to and fro* of existence which at one time allows itself to take corporeal form and at others moves towards personal acts (I am emphasizing – DFMS) (Merleau-Ponty, 1970: 88).

Another prominent thinker of the early 20th century, Ludwig Wittgenstein, highlights another side of the nature-freedom split. In his *Notebooks* (1914-1916) he holds that we are in a certain sense *dependent* and "what we are dependent on we can call God." To this he adds the statement: "There are two godheads: the world and my independent I" (Wittgenstein, 1961:74/75).[21]

The philosophical anthropology of Max Scheler, Adolf Portmann and Arnold Gehlen is guided by the primacy of the freedom motive. Modern (neo-)Darwinism in its genetic determinism (as advanced by Dawkins and others) assigns primacy to the nature motive. The Nobel prize winner, Walter Gilbert (a biochemist from Harvard University), claims that the (Socratic) instruction "know thyself" actually refers to (biological) knowledge of the human "genome."

An opposing view is advanced by Stephen Gould for he believes that "the issue is not universal biology vs. human uniqueness," but "biological potentiality vs. biological determinism" (Gould, 1992:252). *Potentiali-*

---

21. "Es gibt zwei Gottheiten: Die Welt und mein Unabhängiges Ich."

ty here represents the humanistic freedom motive and *determinism* represents the classical humanistic science ideal. Gould rejects the meaningless speculations of socio-biologists and alternatively posits human flexibility encompassing a vast range of potential behaviour. Ultimately Gould aims at maintaining a relative balance between these dialectically opposing poles of the basic motive of nature and freedom.

Karl Jaspers realizes the dead alley present in this dialectical legacy: "Since freedom is only through and against nature, as freedom it must fail. Freedom is only when nature is" (Jaspers, 1948:871).

4.0 Towards an Alternative View

Although the main contours of our preceding analysis focused on the dialectics entailed in ultimate commitments, it was inevitable that alternative ontological stances came into view as well. However, what is particularly striking in all cases is that the ontological views involved all suffered from some or other form of reductionism. For example, in the position taken by Descartes we find a reduction of nature to spatial extension and a reduction of what is typically human to thinking. By and large the dualistic legacy regarding the relationship between body and soul operated with a split between the physical and a non-physical (mind or spirit).

It is clear that throughout this history the human self-hood has been approached from the angle of various *modes of explanation*. The result is that implicitly the human self-hood became dispersed within the diversity of reality – manifest in attempts to explain the mystery of being human merely in terms of one or another aspect of reality.

The history of philosophy and the various academic disciplines witness alternative options, such as a material self, a genetic self, an emotional self, a rational self, a historical self, an interpretative self (*homo symbolicus*), an economic self (*homo economicus*), or a moral self. Sometimes a combination of aspects is employed, such as the well-known characterization of a human person as a *rational-ethical* being.

Increasing research on the human brain inspired reflections of the assumed relationship between the human "mind" and the human brain. Within this field strong reductionistic tendencies surfaced, particularly by those who believe that it is the brain that thinks. Although no one will deny today that thought-activities proceed on the basis of brain-activities, it does not follow that we may assume that it is the brain that is thinking. Speaking and communicating are therefore not brain activities, as pointed out by Janich: "it is not brains that communicate, but interacting persons" (Janich, 2009:73).

Habermas Rejects a Naturalistic Reductionism

Habermas characterizes the current naturalistic determinism which pursues reductionist research strategies aiming at a complete explanation of mental processes by means of observable physiological conditions. According to this view the freedom of the human will is therefore a mere appearance behind which a closed causal connection of neural states, determined by natural laws, hides itself. Yet then he asks the question: "But does the deterministic conception represent a thesis with a natural scientific foundation at all, or does it simply form part of a naturalistic world view resulting from a speculative interpretation of natural scientific knowledge? (Habermas, 2005:156). Elsewhere he asks whether the physiology of our consciousness changes anything of our intuitive awareness of being the accountable author guiding all our actions? (Habermas, 2001:16). His non-reductionist sentiments are evident in his remark: "The scientistic belief in a science which one day in the future not only will broaden our personal self-understanding, but through an objectifying self-description will also *eliminate* it, is not science but bad philosophy" (Habermas, 2001:20).[22]

---

22. "Der szientistische Glaube an eine Wissenschaft, die eines Tages das personalen Selbstverständnis durch eine objektivierende Selbstbeschreibung nich nur ergänzt, sondern *ablöst*,

Implications of a Biblical Perspective

From a biblical perspective, being human is not exhausted by *any* aspect or structure of temporal reality. The radical and central unity of being human transcends both the dimension of aspects and that of entities because it touches the root, the religious centre of a human person, sometimes designated as the *heart*, the *soul* or the *spirit*. We have shown that the traditional dualism of body and soul derives from the reification of opposing clusters of modal functions, as a rule by allocating the natural sides of reality to the (material) body and the norming modes to the (rational) soul.

According to Vollenhoven the biblical sense of "immortality" means "not being subject to the power of death – in the Scriptural sense of this term." Before the first death human immortality is not mentioned and the Bible never speaks of an immortal part of a person (it does not know the expressions "immortal soul" and "immortal spirit"). Moreover, the Bible solely knows of immortality of those who, after their death, are in Christ. Immortality means more than "continue to exist" while "being subject to death" does not mean annihilation (Vollenhoven, 1933 – see the Appendix with the footnotes, note 40). The crucial biblical emphasis on the unity of the whole person (both in the Old and

---

ist nicht Wissenschaft, sondern slechte Philosophie."

New Testaments) is thoroughly discussed by Janse in Chapter VI of his work on *Idols and Creatures* (see Janse, 1938:50-86).

The dualism between "matter" and "spirit" denies the integral coherence both of the various aspects and the various kinds of entities found within the world. Dooyeweerd points out that the "anima rationalis" is merely a theoretical abstraction from the temporal human body. Moreover, it "contradicts the view that the 'intellect' is its essence and that the 'body' is its 'matter' " for "the intellect after all is within this conception not the entire soul." Dooyeweerd proceeds: "In the Aristotelian-Platonic theory of immortality this clearly comes to expression. Here immortality is only reserved for the *nous* – viewed as the intellect purified from all sensitive functions (the rational part of the soul in Plato)" (Dooyeweerd, 1939:203; Dooyeweerd, 2013a:159).

The basic contours of an integral, biblically informed understanding of the human personality therefore requires an account of the coherence between the various modal aspects of reality, of the diverse subject-subject relations and subject-object relations found within them as well as the complex intertwinement of different (sub-)structures within the human body.

Human beings function actively, that is as *subjects*,

within all aspects of reality (see the Sketch preceding the Bibliography – by the author). Each human person is one, occupies space, moves, acts, is alive, is sensitive, identifies and distinguishes, is culturally formative, speaks, is thrifty, is beautiful (or ugly), can be just, loving and trusting (compare the aspects listed in the just-mentioned Sketch).

By contrast, material things only function actively within the aspects of number, space, the kinematic and the physical. In all the post-physical aspects, physical entities have *object*-functions: a diamond, for example, does not live but nonetheless may be present within the habitat of living entities. A diamond is not a sensory subject, but it can be perceived by sensory subjects (animals and humans). A diamond cannot identify and distinguish, but human beings are capable to identify diamonds and distinguish them from whatever is not a diamond. Diamonds are not by nature cultural objects, but human beings can provide them with a cultural shape. They have no lingual ability but do have a name. Diamonds cannot interact socially but may be a status symbol. Surely they cannot be economically active, although they may be pricey. Diamonds are beautiful, can be owned by someone (property right) and may be adored. Finally, once they have been given a particular cultural shape, they are reliable in performing a specific expected function.

The identification of the human body with what is considered to be material (physical) lacks a proper understanding of the fact that within the human body four different entity-structures are intertwined in such a way that each retains its inner sphere of operation while at the same time contributing to the functioning of the entire human body. There is more to the atoms and molecules than what meets the eye! Consider for example the role of iodine within the normal functioning of the thyroid gland.

This gland (the *glandula thyreoidea*) is found around the lower part of the human larynx and the beginning of the wind pipe. It regulates the secretion of the thyroid gland hormone (*thyroxine*) which initiates the exchange of substances throughout the body's cells by influencing the process of oxidative phosphorylation in the mitochondria, an organelle within the cell. These processes are crucial for normal biotic growth as well as emotional and psychic health. Yet iodine has a physical-chemical qualification in respect of its own inner structure. While maintaining this physical structure it is nonetheless said to be *enkaptically* bound within the organic functioning of the thyroid gland.

Dooyeweerd introduces the term *enkaptic* to account for forms of *interlacmement* or *intertwinement* where the inner sphere of operation of what is interlaced is not violated in spite of the fact that at once it renders an external service to the whole of which it is an enkaptic part. Diverse natural and societal entities are designated by Dooyeweerd as individuality-structures.

It is only the thyroid gland that actively (subjectively) functions within the biotic aspect of reality in dependence upon the enkaptically bound iodine responsible for the internal secretion of the thyroid gland hormone. This biotic function in turn plays a foundational enkaptical role within the sensitive sub-structure as well as within the normative functioning of the human being. It is important for a healthy emotional and norm-guided life of human beings. When the thyroid gland is hyperactive it causes excessive energy-use which can generate a faster heartbeat accompanied by a general unease and a heightened nervous sensitivity. The interwoven iodine and thyroid gland therefore indeed operates within the integrated functioning of the entire human being, without sacrificing its inner sphere of operation, which continues to be qualified respectively by the physical-chemical and biotic aspects.

While all the bodily structures of humans have, apart from their enkaptic interweaving, a characteristic internal functional sphere, it is impossible to delimit any one of them in a *morphological* sense, that is, to localize them within any particular *part* of the body. This explains why the foot, the hand or the leg of a human being is never purely physically, biotically or sensorially structured. The entire human personality, embracing all enkaptically interwoven sub-structures, is expressed in every part of the body. Therefore, it is impossible for medical and nursing practice to reduce a person to a purely *biotic entity*.

Initially Dooyeweerd struggled to come to terms with what he eventually designated as the act-structure of the human body. At a certain stage in the development of his thought he opted for the idea that there is a "spiritual" ("geestelijke") structure in which the pre-logical sub-structures are enkaptically bound, but then added the remark that this spiritual structure is qualified by the faith function ("door de geloofsfunctie gequalificeerde ... lichaamsstructuur" – Dooyeweerd, 1940:222).

However, since a human being can successively act under the guidance of diverse normative considerations, it is clear that none of the post-sensory (normative) functions could *qualify* these normed actions all at once. The result was that Dooyeweerd advanced the idea that although the act-structure is the qualifying structure of the human body, it is not qualified in itself (see Dooyeweerd, 2011:165 ff.). Another way to characterize this qualifying act-structure is to say that it is *undifferentiated* (see Dooyeweerd, 2011:175 ff.). He describes "acts" as follows:

> By the word "acts" – differentiated in their basic dimensions of knowing, imagining and willing – I understand those activities which issue from the human selfhood but function within the enkaptic body individuality-structure. Through them, one orients oneself intentionally (i.e., with a purpose) towards states of affairs in temporal reality – or in the world of one's imagination – under the guidance of normative points of view. One internalizes these intentional (or intended) states of affairs by relating them to one's I-ness. Their "innerness" is involved in the intentional character of the "acts" (Dooyeweerd, 2011:148).

Perhaps it would be simpler to avoid the distinction between "inner" and "outer" by simply calling this structure the *normative structure*. Interestingly, during the first few decades of the development of the *Philosophy of the Cosmonomic Idea* both Dooyeweerd and Vollenhoven experimented with the idea of the *functional garb* of a human being (see Vollenhoven, 2005: §93, page 62; Dooyeweerd, 1939:204; Dooyeweerd, 2013a:160). Eventually Dooyeweerd employed his idea of individuality-structures – an approach not shared by Vollenhoven.

The non-reductionist ontology found in the philosophy of Dooyeweerd and Vollenhoven on the one hand acknowledges that the aspects within which human beings actively function are fitted within an unbreakable coherence in such a way that no single one should be elevated above all the others, as it is found in the distorting one-sidedness of well-known isms, such as atomism, holism, physicalism, biologism, psychologism, logicism, historicism, aestheticism, legalism, or moralism.

Elevating something within creation is normally accompanied by depreciating something else – the cause of dialectical oppositions which result in the confusion of the good structure of the creation order with the directional antithesis between good and evil (redemption and sin) – also well-documented in the elevation of the human (intellectual) "soul" (supposedly "good") and the depreciation of the human (material) "body" (supposedly inherently "evil."

A radical biblical perspective rejects every dualism. From the depth perspective of the Christian world view we should realize that we are constantly confronted with the deification of something within creation. Absolutizations like these constantly distort a proper understanding of the human "I-ness" because they rest on an over-evaluation of a well-created part of reality, which at once leads to a depreciation of something else within creation – already a fundamental characteristic of the ancient heresy of Gnosticism. This attitude idolizes (deifies) something within creation – a point of departure of all idolatrous service, which glorifies creatures instead of God.

Before we close our analysis, however, we have to focus briefly on the discussions generated by the idea of *supra-temporality*.

4.3 Supra-Temporality

Vollenhoven and Dooyeweerd consistently subscribed to the distinction between the central (pre-functional or supra-modal) religious root ("heart") of being human and the aspectual diversity within reality. However, Vollenhoven did not accept the idea of *supra-temporality*. Nonetheless, in his *Isagôgè Philosophiae* he does explain that time is not an aspect and also briefly accounts for the appearance of time within all modalities (see Vollenhoven §48; Vollenhoven, 2005:33) – a view equivalent to what Dooyeweerd does in 1940 and 1940a.

In 1968 Vollenhoven mentions that he was initially influenced by Poincaré who believed that the succession of numbers is connected with or founded in the succession of time (Vollenhoven, 1968:3). With reference to the succession of numbers and of time he notes that Dooyeweerd concludes from the temporality of reality that it must then include the arithmetical as well (Vollenhoven, 1968:3). Yet Vollenhoven and Dooyeweerd share the distinction between the heart or soul and the functions (Vollenhoven's preferable mode of expression is to refer to the *pre-functional* heart in this regard). Of course, from a purely logical point of view the acknowledgment of time embracing all aspects (and entities) by itself does not turn this distinction (between modal and supra-modal) into an impasse. An additional argument is required to show this.

In his response to the "marginal" remarks formulated by Van Peursen in respect of Dooyeweerd's *A New Critique of Theoretical Thought*, Dooyeweerd revisited his initial assessment of the central religious dimension as something "supra-temporal." Dooyeweerd holds that we "do transcend time in the center of our existence even though at the same time we are enclosed within time" (Dooyeweerd, 1960:103) and later on in this article he explains that he is not wedded to the term "supra-temporal," for in response to the objection raised by Van Peursen to the term "supra-temporal," he says:

> Now I am not once more going to enter into a discussion regarding the question if it is desirable to call the heart, as the religious centre of human existence,

supra-temporal. It is sufficiently known that amongst the adherents of the *Philosophy of the Cosmonomic Idea* there is no consensus in this regard. Probably the term supra-temporal, with which I never meant a static condition but merely intended to capture a central direction of consciousness transcending cosmic time, can best be replaced by another one (Dooyeweerd, 1960:137).

In 1964 the same issue surfaced in a discussion of the *Annual Meeting* of the philosophical association founded by Vollenhoven and Dooyeweerd. A transcription of this discussion reports that Steen asked Dooyeweerd about the idea of supra-temporality. Dooyeweerd answered that sometimes he can "tear the hair from his head" that he ever used this expression. Nonetheless he continued to hold that the human being, in the centre of its existence, transcends the temporal cosmic order.[23] What is of importance for Dooyeweerd, is the centrality of the human selfhood,

---

23. The transcription reads: "… waar ik soms de haren uit mijn hoofd trek (you understand?), dat ik deze uitdrukking ooit zo gebruikt heb, ik geloof niet dat ik deze uitdrukking ooit zo gebruikt heb. Ik heb wel dit gezegd, dat de mens in het centrum van zijn bestaan de tijdelijke, de kosmische tijdelijke orde te boven gaat. Dat is wel iets anders" (the *Dooyeweerd Archives* available at the "Historische Documentatiecentrum," Free University, Amsterdam – investigated during March, 2006).

in the sense that it cannot be identified with any modal aspect or with any "individuality-structure" – and not the distinction between temporal meaning-diversity and the "supra-temporal heart" *per se*. Already in 1939 one finds formulations that emphasize that the supra-temporal is *experienced*[24] in the deepest core of the human being. Dooyeweerd here also points out that the *awareness* of eternity resides in the human heart by virtue of its createdness.[25]

Throughout *A New Critique of Theoretical Thought* (and elsewhere) Dooyeweerd merely refers to the *central* or *transcendent religious* dimension of creation without necessarily adding the qualification "supra-temporal." In the light of his 1960 and 1964 remarks it is clear that the distinction between temporal and supra-temporal is not crucial for his philosophy. Just recall his remark that he "never meant a static condition but merely intended to capture a central direction of consciousness transcending cosmic time." What is therefore crucial is

---

24. Time only turns into a genuine *problem* "wanneer wij *distantie* tegenover hem kunnen nemen in het boven-tijdelijke, dat wij in het diepst van ons wezen ervaren" ["... when we can take distance to it in the spura-temporal that we experience in the deepest core of our being"] (Dooyeweerd, 1939:1).

25. "De geheele Heilige Schrift leert ons immers, dat het eeuwigheidsbesef aan 's menschen hart is ingeschapen" (Dooyeweerd, 1939:2 note 1).

the distinction between God and creation as well as the centrality of the human selfhood (heart) coupled with the centrality of the core dimension of creation where the ultimate commitment of being human has its seat and from where direction is given to all of life. But this does not entail a dualism between body and soul in its traditional Aristotelian-Thomistic sense (see also Dooyeweerd, 2012:31-36). The distinction between the central religious dimension of creation and the dimensions of modal aspects and concretely existing (natural and social) entities ("individuality-structures") remains valid irrespective of whether they are all seen as temporal or if the central religious dimension is seen as "time-transcending" or "supra-temporal." After all, when Dooyeweerd speaks of a "central direction of consciousness transcending cosmic time" then it is clear that the central direction of the self-hood differs from the nature of the self-hood.

5.0 Concluding Remarks

An integral view of the human person, not succumbing to any dialectical or dualistic view, has to proceed from a non-reductionist ontology entailing the distinctiveness of *structure* and *direction*. The unity and goodness of creation indeed precludes a dualistic understanding of the origin of the universe in which certain parts are elevated and others depreciated. Wolters succinctly states:

> In my view, it ought to be a mark of philosophy which seeks to be as radical as the Bible that it renounces this whole enterprise, and simply accepts, as a point of departure, that every creature of God is good, and that sin and salvation are matters of opposing religious direction, not of good and evil sectors of the created order. All aspects of created life and reality are in principle equally good, and all are in principle equally subject to perversion and renewal (Wolters, 1981:10-11).

Sketch
(by author)

The Human Being - a Religious Personality

Enkaptic structural intertwinements of the human body with subject functions in all aspects

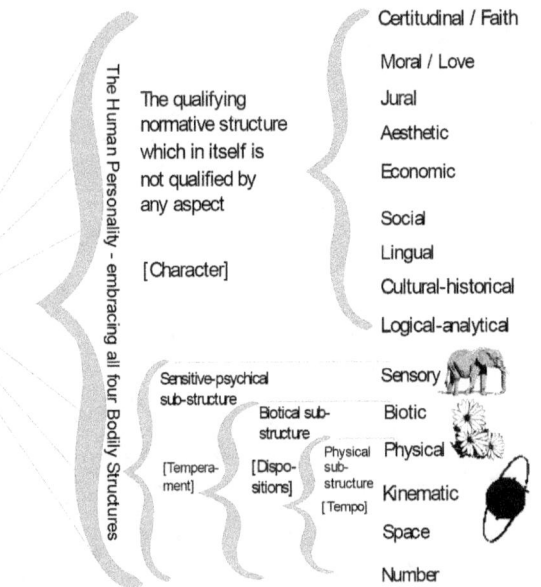

Aspects

- Certitudinal / Faith
- Moral / Love
- Jural
- Aesthetic
- Economic
- Social
- Lingual
- Cultural-historical
- Logical-analytical
- Sensory
- Biotic
- Physical
- Kinematic
- Space
- Number

The qualifying normative structure which in itself is not qualified by any aspect

[Character]

Sensitive-psychical sub-structure

Biotical sub-structure

Physical sub-structure

[Temperament] [Dispositions] [Tempo]

The Human Personality - embracing all four Bodily Structures

The human heart (the religious root of human existence)

The human heart, soul or spirit - understood in its radical, central and total sense - is the religious root of the human personality transcending its embodiment in the four enkaptically interwoven structures

Enkapsis concerns the interlacement of two differently-natured structures such that each retains its inner sphere of operation. The constitutive physical configuration of living things does not lose its physical-chemical qualification when it functions within living entities. Such entities are functioning enkaptically – that is, retaining their physically qualified nature – within living things. Similarly, the biotic organs and the sensory sub-structures of the human body are enkaptically interwoven in the total bodily existence of a person.

LITERATURE

Aristotle. 2001. 'The Basic Works of Aristotle'. Edited by Richard McKeon with an Introduction by C.D.C. Reeve. (Originally published by Random House in 1941). New York: The Modern Library.

Aquinas, Th. 1945. 'Basic Writings of Saint Thomas Aquinas', Vol. I en II, Edited by A.C. Pegis, New York: Random house.

Aquinas, Th. 1982. 'Summe gegen die Heiden'. Edited and translated by Karl Albert and Paulus Engelhardt, Second Volume. Darmstadt: Wissenschaftliche Buchgesellschaft.

Augustine, A. 1966. 'Confessiones' (Confessions), Translated with an Introduction by Pine-Coffin: R.S. Harmondsworth: Penguin Books.

Augustine, A. 1982. 'De Genesi ad litteram' (The literal meaning of Genesis), Translated from the Latin and annotated by John Hammond Taylor. New York N.Y.: Newman cop.

Bishop, S. and Kok, J. 2013. 'On Kuyper. A Collection of Readings on the Life, Work & Legacy of Abraham Kuyper'. Edited by Steve Bishop and John H. Kok.

Dordt: Dordt College Press.

Bos, A.P. 2003. 'The Soul and its Instrumental Body, A Reinterpretation of Aristotle's Philosophy of Living Nature'. Leiden-Boston: Brill.

Dooyeweerd, H. 1939. 'Kuyper's Wetenschapsleer'. In: Philosophia Reformata 4(4):193-232.

Dooyewerd, H. 1940. 'The Problem of Time in the Philosophy of the Cosmonomic Idea I', Philosophia Reformata, Year 5, 3rd Quarter, pp.160-192.

Dooyewerd, H. 1940a. 'The Problem of Time in the Philosophy of the Cosmonomic Idea II', Philosophia Reformata, Year 5, 4th Quarter, pp.193-234.

Dooyeweerd, H. 1960. 'Van Peursen's critische vragen bij "A New Critique of Theoretical Thought",' Philosophia Reformata, 25(1&2) 97-150.

Dooyeweerd, H. 2011. Reformation and Scholasticism in Philosophy. Volume III. Philosophy of Nature and Philosophical Anthropology. Grand Rapids: Paideia Press.

Dooyeweerd, H. 2012. Reformation and Scholasticism in Philosophy. Volume I, The Greek Prelude. Grand Rapids: Paideia Press.

Dooyeweerd, H. 2012a. The Struggle for a Christian Politics. Grand Rapids: Paideia Press.

Dooyeweerd, H. 2012b. 'Roots of Western Culture. Pagan,

Secular, and Christian Options'. Grand Rapids: Paideia Press.

Dooyeweerd, H. 2013. 'Reformation and Scholasticism in Philosophy'. Volume II, The Philosophy of the Cosmonomic Idea and the Scholastic Tradition in Christian Thought. Grand Rapids: Paideia Press.

Dooyeweerd, H. 2013a. 'Kuyper's Philosophy of Science'. In: Bishop & Kok, 2013:153-178.

Everson, S. (Ed.) 1991. 'Psychology. Companions to ancient thought 2'. Cambridge: Cambridge University Press.

Fischer, E.P. 1996. 'Aristoteles, Einstein & Co'. München: Piper.

Gould, S.J. 1992. Reflections in Natural History. Ever Since Darwin. New York: W.W. Norton & Company.

Habermas, J. 2001. Glauben und Wissen. Frankfurt am Main: Suhrkamp.

Habermas, J. 2005. 'Zwischen Naturalismus und Religion'. Frankfurt am Main: Suhrkamp.

Happ, H. 1971. 'Studien zum aristotelischen Materie-Begriff'. Berlin: Walter de Gruyter.

Hartman, E. 1977. 'Substance, Body, and Soul'. Princeton: Princeton University Press.

Janich, P. 2009. 'Kein neues Menschenbild. Zur Sprache

der Hirnforschung'. Frankfurt am Main: Suhrkamp.

Janse, A. 1938. 'Van Idolen en Schepselen'. Kampen: Kok.

Jaspers, K. 1948. 'Philosophie'. Berlin: Springer Verlag.

Kant, I. 1787. 'Kritik der reinen Vernunft', 2nd Edition (references to CPR B). Hamburg: Felix Meiner edition (1956).

Kremer, K. 1971. 'Die neuplatonische Seinsphilosophie und ihre Wirkung auf Thomas von Aquin'. Second Edition. Leiden: Brill.

Manser, G. 1935. 'Das Wesen des Thomismus'. Freiburg: F. Rütschi.

Mead, G.H. 1945: 'The Philosophy of the Act', 2nd edition, Chicago: Chicago University Press.

Merleau-Ponty, M. 1970. 'Phenomenology of Perception'. Translated by Colin Smith, 5th Edition. London: Routledge & Kegan Paul.

Rousseau, J.J. 1975. 'Du Contrat Social et Autres Oeuvres Politiques'. Paris: Editions Garnier Fréres.

Sertillanges, A.D. 1954 (second Edition). 'Der Heilige Thomas von Aquin', Translated from the French by Robert Grosche. Köln: Hegner.

Ter Horst. G.J. 2008. 'De ontbinding van de substantie, Een deconstructie van de beginselen van vorm en materie in de ontology en de kenleer van Thomas van

Aquino'. Delft: Uitgeverij Eburon.

Thompson, M. 2012. 'Understand Philosophy of Mind'. London: Hodder Edcucation.

Tönnies, F. 1912. 'Thomas Hobbes, der Mann und der Denker'. 2nd enl. ed.

Osterwieck/Harz: Zickfeldt.

Tredennick, H. 1966 (Translator). 'Plato, The Last Days of Socrates'. Hardmondsworth: Penguin Books.

Verdenius, W.J. and Waszink, J.H. 1968. 'Aristotle on coming to be and passing away'. Leiden: E.J. Brill.

Vollenhoven, D.H. 1933. 'Het Calvinisme en de Reformatie van de Wijsbegeerte'. Amsterdam: H.J. Paris.

Vollenhoven, D.H. 1968. 'Problemen van de tijd in onze kring'. Presentation to the Circle of Amsterdam (Association for Reformational Philosophy – Chairperson Dooyeweerd).

Text based upon a tape recording by J. Kraay, checked and corrected in a few instances by Vollenhoven, with a six point summary written by Vollenhoven himself (added on page 8).

Vollenhoven, D.H. 2005. 'ISAGÔGÈ PHILOSPHIAE. Introduction to Philosophy'. Edited by John Kok and Anthony Tol. Dordt: Dordt College Press.

Von Fritz, K. 1984. 'Beiträge zu Aristoteles'. Berlin: Walter de Gruyter.

Wittgenstein, L. 1961 (Eds. G.H. Von Wright, G.E.M. Anscombe with an English translation by G.E.M. Anscombe). 'Notebooks 1914-1916'. Oxford: Basil Blackwell.

Wolters, A. 1981. 'Facing the Perplexing History of Philosophy'. In: Journal for Christian Scholarship, 17(4):1-31.

ABOUT THE AUTHOR

D.F.M. Strauss served as Head of the Department of Philosophy at the University of Free State (Bloemfontein, South Africa) and Dean of the Faculty of Humanities (1998-2001). He is the General Editor of the *Collected Works* of the Dutch legal scholar and philosopher, Herman Dooyeweerd and is one of five Outstanding Professors at the University of the Free State. Apart from 15 independent publications, 36 international conference papers and 20 contributions to multi-author works, he has published more than 230 articles in national and international journals, spread over 12 different scientific subject areas.

PAIDEIA MONOGRAPHS

Other Titles (2020–):

The Development of Calvinism in North America
H. Evan Runner

Point Counter Point
H. Evan Runner

The Radical Christian Facing Today's Political Malaise
H. Evan Runner

The Analogical Concepts
Herman Dooyeweerd

The Concept of Sovereignty in Modern Jurisprudence and Political Science
Herman Dooyeweerd

The Criteria of Progressive and Reactionary Tendencies in History
Herman Dooyeweerd

The Secularization of Science
Herman Dooyeweerd

**Looking for more?
Visit www.paideiapress.ca**

www.ingramcontent.com/pod-product-compliance
Lightning Source LLC
Chambersburg PA
CBHW052030290426
44112CB00014B/2454